Your Cleaner Hates You
and other poems

Cathi Rae

Cathi Rae asserts the moral right to be identified as the author of this work under the Copyright, Designs and Patents Act 1988.

All rights reserved. No part of this book may be reproduced or used in any manner whatsoever without the express written permission of the publisher, except for brief quotations in a book review.

Published in the United Kingdom by

Coalville C.A.N. Community Publishing
Marlborough Square,
Coalville,
Leicestershire,
England
LE67 3TU

https://coalvilleccp.uk

First Published in 2019
Second Edition (revised)

ISBN 978-1-9174293-8-2

10 9 8 7 6 5 4 3 2 1

INTRODUCTION

It's not often that a poet has the opportunity to revisit an existing publication. This 2024 edition of Your Cleaner Hates You includes new poems and revisions to the original collection.

I owe a huge debt of gratitude to all the spoken word promoters and performers without whom there would be no spoken word scene, thank you to all of you who have allowed me to perform or who have shared work that reminds me just how powerful poetry can be.

Huge thanks to Constantine and everyone at Coalville C.A.N Community Publishing, for this opportunity to re-publish this collection.

Contents

1. Your Cleaner Hates You
2. Dogs… And People
3. Things That Have Happened / Will Happen / May Not Happen
4. Love *Slash* Not Love
5. The Chi Chi Trilogy
6. To Do and Not To Do
7. Newer Poems

[1]

Your Cleaner Hates You

YOUR CLEANER HATES YOU

Not of course in the way she hates Crocs,
Jacob Rees Mogg or the kind of people
who talk about going for a cheeky Nando's.

But, make no mistake, your cleaner hates you.

And just because she knows the names of your dog,
guinea pigs and husband and remembers
to ask about your son, studying what was it?
forensic physiology and photography
at Wolverhampton, Warwick or DMU...
don't be fooled, your cleaner hates you.

Sometimes, your cleaner wonders
what exactly it is you do all day,
given that you have a woman to clean your house
and a woman to iron your clothes and another,
slightly younger posher woman to walk your dog.

Oh, they hate you too.

You tell your cleaner that you have 'projects'
on the go as you waft to your study on the third floor,
your room of own's own.

What you don't do up there   ever
is bring down the multitude of mouldy
and malodorous mugs,
some homage to a long-gone undergraduate lifestyle
and your cleaner would like you to know
that emptying an ashtray
into a wicker wastepaper basket is exactly the same

as not emptying it all
but with additional hoovering work.

Your cleaner hates you.

Your cleaner has flicked through
your expensive moleskin-bound journal
and quite frankly her advice would be
not to give up your day job,
if of course you had a day job to give up.

Your cleaner hates your poetry.

Your cleaner hates the rumpled crumpled
used up tissues you leave in your unmade bed.

She hates the ring of pubic pelt around your bath,
but at least she knows for sure
that you're not a natural blonde.

But most of all your cleaner hates the notes:

The – *"House in a bit of a state today,
please work your usual magic, kiss kiss"*

The – *"If you get time today,
can you empty all the kitchen cupboards,
clean them and put everything back,
but you know, just better, kiss, kiss, kiss"*

The – *"Don't bother coming for the next 2 weeks,
we're away, kiss"*

Come the glorious revolution,
you will find yourself

not with your back against the wall,
instead, you will be issued with an official cleaner car,
ancient, prone to make noises so terrifyingly
potentially expensive that you will be forced to drive
everywhere with the stereo cranked up
as loud as you can bear,
while you mumble prayers
to some god of pauper's transportation.

"Please just let the car last a few more months..."

And you will get to wear cleaner clothes,
ill-fitting grey joggers and a sweatshirt
full of holes where neat bleach has burnt
through fabric to meet soft bare flesh.

Then, then you will become your cleaner's cleaner.

And your cleaner, your ex-cleaner
will look you in the eye
and she will know that you hate her, but actually,
actually, your cleaner, your ex-cleaner...

Your ex-cleaner won't give a flying fuck.

THERE IS MORE TO YOUR CLEANER
THAN MEETS YOUR EYE

This one gets up at 5am,
runs as fast and far as lungs and heart can bear,
revels in the recognition
from other early morning pavement pounders,
then puts on the uniform of tabard,
bleach-stained leggings,
becomes invisible again.

This one knows the name of every star
that's in the sky, and more than that
can tell you why they are so named,
but has spent so long on hands and knees
she fears she may have lost the knack of looking up.

This one's boyfriend's banged up again,
working double shifts
she curates a collection of child-care
so complicated, so tenuous,
that in a gallery it would be labelled web
or DNA of everyday.

This one says she's lucky.
In a refugee camp far away
at 15, 16,
the soldiers said she was too old to rape
so, mostly, she was left alone.

This one speaks 5 languages
including yours,
so, knows exactly what your husband
and his mates make of her arse

when she bends down to scrub your skirting boards.
Laser jets from lowered lids,
if looks could kill.

This one holds a broken bird,
a touch so light
it's as if her hands were wings,
and not these red and swollen things.
Fingerprints burnt off by bleach;
convenient, she always thinks,
should she start a new career
as master thief.

And this one,
this one's writing poetry,
verse as vicious as vipers,
mouth so acidic it makes diamonds bleed.
This one's writing poetry.

There's more to your cleaner than you will ever see.

16 REASONS TO BE NICE TO YOUR CLEANER

1. She knows what lives behind your sofa.

2. She knows what goes on behind closed doors.

3. She could, if she wanted to,
   clean your toilet with your toothbrush.
   She doesn't, but she could.

4. She knows you wear the same pyjamas for a week,
   or is it two?

5. She knows who takes anti-depressants
   and who should, really, really should.

6. She could, if she wanted to, rewrite your magnetic
   fridge poetry into a rant of Polish obscenities, she
   could, but actually she doesn't have the time.

7. She knows whose son is drinking cider and
   whose son is dealing weed.

8. She knows whose daughter keeps a razor blade in a
   tiny tin under an almost still fluffy, gnarled greying
   Bunnykins.

9. She could stop for a moment and think about what it would be like to sit at a scrubbed (by her, of course) pine table with Pilates pals and eat lemon drizzle cake, she could, but she knows that you monitor the hoover as it trundles from room to room, so she could, but she dare not.

10. She knows you didn't make the lemon drizzle cake.

11. She knows you did eat 3 packets of crisps, 2 large Mars Bars and a gluten free chocolate cake in bed this week.

12. She could tell you that her children got far better A-level results than yours, but she won't. She guards her privacy. The knowing and the knowledge is one-way street.

13. She knows you are £234.57 overdrawn after payday.

14. She knows that you shop in Aldi now, but carry it home in your Cath Kidston jute shopping bags.

15. She could make a fuss about the underpayment, the *didn't have any change,* the *will sort it out next week,*

but she won't. Instead, she has taken to letting the
Hoover run on, un-minded, while she stares
out of the windows, stealing back time.

16. She knows it won't be long now
 until you are the one picking up your
 husband's toenail clippings from the bedside table,
 scrubbing your own pine table, washing the plates
 your children leave under beds until they fester,
 become concrete, difficult to clean
 and then when she meets you, in the street, sometime
 next week, next year, maybe,

Your ex-cleaner,
well, she will be very nice to you indeed.

[2]

Dogs...and People

I'VE GOT NOTHING AGAINST DOG PER SE

The moment the words are out of her mouth,
she wishes she hadn't said them.

They hang in the air, too heavy for their actual content,
she particularly regrets the Latin tag,
what was she thinking of?

There is a pause, she sips her latte,
extra shot, two sugars
and wonders how to get this conversation
back on track.

And now from nowhere,
she is actually impersonating
the talking pug from YouTube
"iiiaaaaaa wuubbbbb yooooouuuuu"
she even manages the little howl at the end.

There is another pause.

"I mean, it's not like they talk very well or anything"

her daughter stares at her
torn midway between horror and her default position
of mild derision for the mother who never ever gets it.

They both look down at their cake plates.

The mother cannot stop herself

*"it would be so much better
if they said something interesting".*

The daughter buries herself in her iPod playlist,
she is prepared to give her mother half an ear,
usually that's enough to avoid accusations of rudeness,
the litany about the youth of today,
but also ensures that she doesn't really
have to pay any attention.

There is another pause,
the mother says she wants to take the daughter's photo,
but the girl hides her face in her jacket,
refuses to pose.

There is another longer pause and then defeated,
she puts the camera away.

"when I get a dog, I'm going to teach it to say I love you"
says the daughter defiantly.

Fearing the answer, the mother is too afraid to ask why.

They stand up and leave the café together.

JOSIAH AND HIS HAIR

Josiah and his silent friend
are walking with me through the meadows
and he is telling me the story of his hair.
This hair is story-worthy,
part flat top, part dreadlocks,
no medusa coils.
If these dreadlocks were alive
they would be smiling, sunbathing, sleepy snakes.

Josiah says:
"When I was little, I had an afro,
combed it every day.
Discovered that the big girls from the big school
liked to stroke my hair,
discovered that I liked that too".

And Josiah says,
"Then I got a flat top,
urban flavour,
sharp, hard edged"

And Josiah says,
"My grandmother,
buffalo soldier all her life,
wore her dreads wrapped in fabric from home,
flashes of red and yellow and green.
My grandmother died".

And Josiah says,
*"So, these locks remind me
that my grandmother is always with me".*

And when I look,
I see his shoulders are
broad enough to bear this burden.

I CANNOT WRITE A NOVEL TODAY

I cannot write a novel today because…

1. My friend is writing poetry for gerbils and I need to watch the letter box for the manuscript, small and brown, a forgettable butterfly of verse.

2. The towels in my airing cupboard cry out to be arranged not just by size and colour, but fluffiness, fraying and the frisson of pleasure they give against warm damp skin.

3. Somewhere, out there, the perfect shoes exist, red, patent leather, kitten heeled, whimsical lacing and my feet are restless with longing.

4. The sofa groans with undiscovered hidden treasures, chocolate coins, half smoked cigarettes, a tiny china rabbit. I feel the urge for urban archaeology.

5. The dog seems depressed, not in touch with his inner-wolf. I try to cheer him up by baying at the moon, it's the least I can do.

6. Somebody has updated their status, a photograph of mashed potatoes, onion gravy, steaming sausages. I need to comment , *yum yum.*

7. The horse needs me to stand, one foot resting on a gate, my chin against the sun warmed metal of the fastening, watching her eat grass.

8. The ducks are all in disarray, facing the wrong way on the bathroom shelf, if ignored disaster will certainly follow.

9. The biscuit tin contains only cut-price own-label digestives; nobody can expect creativity on such poor fare.

10. There are blue pens in the black pen jar and felt tips with the wrong colour lids and Duplo in the Lego box and the My Little Ponies are missing their mane combs.

    I cannot write a novel today.

DEBT

And afterwards, saved from jumping,
from falling,
he looks directly at her.
"I will always be in your debt"
he says, and she nods,
appraising the truth of this statement.

At first it is easy,
a request to mend a dripping tap,
chop wood for her fire,
drive her and a sickly pet to the vets.

He is happy to help,
after all he is in her debt.

But the tasks become more complex,
long journeys to collect objects,
she says
she cannot live without.
Heavy manual labour around her home,
jobs that take up more and more
of his free time.

He considers refusing,
but the pause she leaves
after each request,
reminds him that
there is a debt to be paid.

And then of course, there are the calls,
late at night,
rambling into silence

or diatribes about the unfairness of her life.

He begins to dread the sound of his phone.

He makes his preparations,
travels to the beach,
weighs his pockets down with stones
and walks towards the water.
He feels only relief, release.

He's made sure
that she's out of town this weekend.

WHEN JAMIE BECOMES BECKI

When Jamie becomes Becki,
he feels lighter,
dancing becomes a joy,
not a chore.
Outfits chosen, un-chosen,
finally discarded
in the tiny back bedroom
where nobody goes except him –
and of course her.

When Jamie becomes Becki,
he still likes to drink pints,
likes how the amber light reflects
onto her sharp red nails,
sometimes wishes
that drinks are served in two-pint mugs.

Wishes that her hands could be dwarfed
as they wrap around the glass,
but shrugs, makes the best of things,
her Pandora bracelet tapping against the rim,
chink, chink, chink.

When Jamie becomes Becki,
it is enough in itself.
Enough for him, enough for her,
no endgame except the possibility
of near seduction in forgiving light,
the possibility of almost passing.

I AM WATCHING THE SWANS
WITH SHANE MACGOWAN

I am standing with Shane, safe in the shadow of the Martello
tower, built to warn the invaders, the interlopers, that others
might come too, blown across the grey sea,
with their own plans to take this poor land.

We are watching the swans, Children of Lir, huddled in the
harbour, buffeted against the jetty. Their plumage,
snow-white, bone-white against the customary grey, brown of
the Irish sea, interlopers themselves and alongside them, other
outsiders. These owners of the yachts, playthings of the
playboys of the western world, or at least the western coasts.

These boats belong somewhere else, somewhere with azure
seas, skies that blend, fall from other shades of blue into the
gentle swell, not this landscape of hard lines and cold breezes.

Shane discourses: poetry, womanizing,
the arts of falconry and warfare.
We walk in the footsteps of writers and warriors, taking the
waters, but not the water of life because Shane is drying out,
drying up, moving towards the years of silence.

I learnt to swim in the other harbour, concrete wall
built to trap the waves and in water so dark that we could not
see the bottom. So, we learn to swim, a lesser terror than
sinking into water we knew had no ending, no sanctuary for
feet, cold-clenched, searching our safe harbour.

We never expected to find this sea-swimming pleasurable,
in water so cold it would
"knock the very breath out of ye"

and from homes where the threat to
"knock the very breath out of ye, see if I won't"
was commonplace, so the sea held no fear for us.

This cold, a rightful punishment for pleasure,
catechism reinforced,
"Who made the world?" "God made the world"

The Italian chipper, our occasional destination, wrapped in
cardigans and anoraks. Our knees and lips
blue from over-immersion in the sea.

These chips, our reward for childhood bravery,
child stoicism. We ate them, huddled into ourselves
against the constant winds.
The taste somehow more delicious the colder we were.

And then, we walked past the Amusement arcade,
because nice children don't go there, licking the tang of salt,
sea salt, chip salt from our fingers as the purple faded
from our knees, our lips.

I wonder what Shane looked at, that winter when the sea and
sky met, bands of grey and brown and dirty white, a million
miles from the plumage of those swans, rocked against the
winter waves.

I wonder if he looked out to sea or turned inland.

I am standing in the shelter of the Martello tower,
taking refuge from the storm, one eye on the horizon,
grey and brown and white.

Watching for interlopers.

BEST ROAD TRIP EVER

The younger dog is puzzled
all this activity
bears the hallmark of a day out
an adventure   a road trip
leads collected
dog bags discovered
keys lost
keys found
he positions himself at the front door
ensuring he is first into the car

but
unaccountably   today he is left behind

home alone
he stands at the window
nose pressed against the glass
confident that a mistake has been made
an error occurred
a wrong to be righted

today is one-woman
one dog
one-way road trip

you let her sit in the front seat
open the window
in case she wants to stand on tippy paws
to hurl abuse at other dogs in other cars

she is tired
sighs   curls up like a kitten
perks up when you open a bag of treats
before you even reach the end of your street

you hand feed her pieces of bite sized chicken
cheese   salami   all the good stuff
and she sighs again
but this time with piggy-greed

in the car park you sit   engine running
while you rub her belly and she   tailless
wags her whole body in pleasure
while you eat the final sliver of cheese
wish that you could freeze this moment forever

the waiting room is empty
first appointment of the day
candle already alight
so you wait   stroke velvet soft ears
push back the inevitable tsunami of tears

not now   not here

and afterwards
when the vet tells you
that you can collect her on Thursday
you look at his face   his lips
can't understand what he's trying to say
until it dawns on you
he means the box of dog-dust
and not her at all

at home   the younger dog is pleased to see you
covers you in dog breath kisses
invites you to a game of bark   nip   run
it is only hours later
after his careful examination
of the garden   the dog beds
and the rooms upstairs
that he finally stands at the front door
stares at you
confident that a mistake has been made
an error occurred
a wrong to be righted.

BE MORE DOG

Be more dog they say
so
I'm shedding language like fur
clawing only to words
that give shape and meaning
to the day
and I'm learning to tilt my head to one side
when you speak   showing interest
although frankly I only get about half what you say

I won't judge by colour of skin
or the cut of your jib
but whether when we meet
you come down to my level
tell me I'm beautiful
offer something delicious to eat

Be more dog they say
so
I'll make as much noise as I want,
and you can't make me shush
and if I'm scared   I'll show it

Left alone for too long
I may make a mess of things
and this may not be a figure of speech

Be more dog they say
so
I'll turn my belly to the sun
and my face to the sky
and fit seven years of living
into each twelve months
because when you're a dog
time flies

Be more dog they say
so
I'll eat when I'm hungry
and eat when I'm full
walk straight past those mirrors
and if I'm with you
well
I'll just make you look more cool

Be more dog.

RESCUE ME

This is for Ryan and Niko (and the dogs of course)

The Polish dog is old
a little moth-eaten, shabby around her seams
she resembles nothing less
than a much-loved greying toy

My dogs are small, sometimes overawed
by the rumbustious play of bigger beasts
but they enjoy her undemanding company
so sometimes we walk together
the Polish dog, the Polish boy and us

He says:
"She is shy"

He says:
"My stepfather used to beat her"

(and I see him choosing not to go there, not today)

He says:
*"But if you give her time and space
allowing her to set the pace   she will stand near
and let you pet her"*

And when we stop   so that she can rest,
she does just that
head just reaching to his knees
leaning in
milky eyes fixed upon his face

My dogs are bored now
cast around for excitement
see Indi explode through the park gates
Indi spent the first six months of her life in a room
because no-one seemed to know that dogs need
walks   fresh air   and other dogs

A different outfit every day
Instagram sensation   many likes not much love
finally rescued and rehomed to the yoga teacher
Indi   making up for lost time
everyday a birthday

We walk together and the boys lean into each other
with an easy intimacy
say something I don't quite catch

And later the yoga teacher says
"We are together"

He says
"We met here, on this park, because of the dogs"

He says
"We are happy"

And it is a tiny everyday miracle
the dogs, the boys, the park
but blink, blink and you might miss it.

[3]

Things That Have Happened / Will Happen / May Not Happen

FIRE-WATCHING

My grandfather cycles at a careful, deliberate pace,
too fast and the dynamo will make the bike lights burn too
bright, too slow and they will flicker,
falter, fail, no light matter in war-darkened Dublin.

My grandfather is going fire-watching.
All night he will stand, binoculars in hand,
surveying the sky.

His war-quality woollen muffler
chafes the back of his neck.
A scarf has been knitted, badly,
by the family's itinerant maid.

This same woman, who each day
will swaddle my mother in her shawl,
a shawl that smells of cheap tobacco, porter, peat.
A smell my mother still remembers almost 90 years on.

At the end of this uneventful shift,
my grandfather will cycle home but this time faster,
as light creeps over the Wicklow hills,
with a final delicious freewheel down Roebuck Rd
and then a sharp left into his own drive.

In daytime, there are drills, alarms sounded,
all clears given. Dubliners, least herdable people
in the world look up. They all have cousins in London,
Birmingham, Coventry, know what the skies can bring.

But, secure in their neutrality, they shrug,
agree that Hitler is a terrible auld eejit,
go back to daily living.

My grandmother sniffs,
sees these drills as showing off.
She goes about her daily business,
queues for jam in which raspberry pips have been
replaced with chips of wood and where no-one
recognises the names of fish at the fishmongers.

He swears they taste like plaice:
they never do.

My grandfather missed
the one night of air-based action.
A German bomber
off path, off plan,
misjudged its route,
tried to jettison the contents
of their bomb bays
into Dublin bay,
misjudged again
took out a row of terraced houses.

Decades later, I lie at his feet,
unravelling knots in a Persian rug.
I clutch my newest Enid Blyton
to my chest, clutch,
but don't read because
I'm trying to make it last.
Even babies of war babies
know the importance of rationing pleasure.

My grandfather's regret
at missing his one chance
of heroism is palpable, even to me.
My grandmother, she's heard it all before,
sniffs and in the absence of any help these days,
goes off to make a pot of tea.

I know I shouldn't, really shouldn't,
but like any addict,
I can convince myself that this time it will be
alright, and if it isn't,
I can easily retune to
Classic FM, Smooth Radio,
lose myself in dance hits of the 90s.

But instead, I'm listening to Radio 4
and a clear-eyed child telling me
that I should panic
about climate change,
panic as if my own house
were on fire
or worry about insect extinction,
antibiotic resistance.

And I wish I had my grandfather's binoculars,
wish I felt their heavy weight of certainty,
wished like him I believed
that this is a world worth fighting for.

Their faces say that we know that we're part of history
and they are watching Notre Dame burn.
Half a world away,
smaller less important churches are burning too.

Another sort of priceless artifact inside,
children dressed in Easter Sunday best
frocks with sticky-out skirts,
gleaming patent shoes.
And some are carrying small baskets of painted eggs.

It's best, I find, to not think about those painted eggs.

In this war there are no drills, no all-clear sounded.
Sometimes, like those people back in Dublin Bay,
it's just poor luck,
wrong time, wrong place.

And I wish we all had my grandfather's binoculars.
All believed with him that this is a world
worth fighting for.

We are all firewatchers now.

CRACKED

You thought this cup would last forever
Victorian bone china
so fine the rim had a ring like a bell
and you were careful
used it sparingly
enveloped it in tissue paper
and bubble wrap
but not enough

You failed to see the flaw
that threatened form
until one day it cracked
left you holding two perfectly imperfect halves
and you dropped   hit the ground
part shock
part moderate scald

But it's hard to keep your footing
when you're already on thin ice
and it's not the shiny stuff you need to fear
the stuff that says   be careful
slipping hazard here
it's the other stuff
the sneaky stuff that takes you unaware
that makes you less than biped
and even when you clamber up
you're not the same
you've suffered some sea change

But it's hard to keep your footing
when you're already on thin ice.

Not everything has a warning light
even things that should
and anyway   they're easy to ignore
to keep on going or
convince yourself on sleepless nights that
somehow everything will be alright

But it's hard to keep your footing
when you're already on thin ice
and every time you fall
you come back somehow less
tissue scars on tissue paper skin so thin
that every jolt will make you bleed
and muscle-memory-pain reminds you that
you will
you will
you will
fall down again

And it's easy to lose your footing when
you're already on thin ice.

[4]

Love *Slash* Not Love

A POEM ON THE IMPORTANCE OF CAREFUL MEASUREMENT PROR TO COMMITTING TO OWNERSHIP

We went to Brighton to buy a bed
new couple yes
but hardly love's young dream

But

Still in need of extra space for languid lounging,
endless pots of tea
love will find a way we said

So, failed to measure car or bed
and failed again
forced to leave it there beside the sea

And even if we'd brought it back
nowadays it would be full of me
and a pack of snoring dogs

But

Sometimes I do wonder that if we'd found
that special way whether we'd still be together
if only for the sake of the furniture.

THIS IS NOT A LOVE SONG

But
you make art and music and good bread
and never forget that I don't like butter
so on picnics my sandwiches are sliced separately,
wrapped differently ensuring that only I get to
enjoy their delicious dryness

   And this is not a love song

But
as a DJ, you kept your head down
Mujahideen hat just visible above the decks
not really a
'Hands In The Air Like You Just Don't Care' kind of guy

But,
Just occasionally, if it was going well,
you would risk a smile and then a quick one two
one two three soft shoe shuffle

   And this is not a love song

But
when my daughter was tiny new
you held her
fitting perfectly into your cupped palms,
not a father never a father
bound to her with ties other than blood,
maybe better

   And this is not a love song

But
you have learnt to slow down
 to keep pace with your father
learnt to bite back irritation when
you have the same conversation
for the third or fourth time today
learnt to cook meals where the meat and vegetables
are clearly delineated on the plate

    And this is not a love song

But
over the years you have
supported my attempts at dressage mediocrity
scouted backgrounds for photo shoots
to meet my social media neediness
and always   always   always
preview horror films to check that I can take them.

    And this is not a love song

But

    This is not a love song.

THE SADDEST THING

This thing.

This thing is the saddest thing.

This is sadder than the face my dog pulls
when a bigger dog steals her tennis ball
and runs away with it.

This is sadder than the time someone told me
I was a poor friend, and my first thought was,
Well, no more late-night drama laden
phone calls from you then.

Sadder than my mother's fridge,
a neat line of pale blue saucers,
each containing a tablespoon of leftover lunch
and in the fridge door, five unopened cartons of milk,
just in case.

This is sadder than when at 17, 18, 19,
your heart broken for the first time,
you lay on the bed, quite convinced that you would die,
because who could endure such pain.

Sadder even, than when at 40, 50, 60,
veteran of multiple failures of heart,
you know all too well that you will survive
this break and the next and the next.

This is sadder than food banks.
Sadder than my neighbour, beginning to lose
language, beginning to feel meaning slipping away.

This is sadder than the boy in the doorway,
his dog wrapped in a coat and a duvet,
snug as a bug in a rug,
but when I look down,
he is wearing shoes, but no socks.

This is the very saddest thing

This is the hearse,
and this is the coffin that doesn't fill it.
All the flowers and helium balloons and teddies
in the world cannot erase this space,
cannot fill this gap, cannot hide this hole.

This is the very, very saddest thing

And then the lights change,
and it turns left,
I execute a clumsy right-hand manoeuvre.
it's hard to drive well when you're crying
for someone else's saddest thing.

VALENTINE'S DAY

It's Valentines Day
and the traffic is at a standstill
gridlocked
we're going nowhere
and I'm tapping

no   actually I'm punching
the steering wheel
"come on, come on, come on"
as if my voice alone
can make movement happen

it's Valentines Day
and all over my network
Bunny Bookins is wishing Mr Fluffy
a really special day
and Kevin is wondering
if you want to play
hide the carrot   later

my texts are terser
*"I'm on my way, I'm coming,
please wait, just wait"*

it's Valentines Day
and every song on the radio
is a fucking love song
and now I'm starting to sob
those shoulder-shaking
snot-making sobs

and I'm seriously considering
just driving down the hard shoulder
*"I'm sorry officer, it was an emergency
and besides it's Valentines Day"*

the man in the stationary van next to me
has had enough time now
to see that something's not right
so he gets out   taps on the window
asks if I'm ok

and I look at him
my hair uncombed   rat-tailed
snail trail tracks of tears
mascara on my chin
I nod and smile and tell him I'm fine

it's Valentines Day
and finally we're moving,
a miracle
and I make a 40-minute journey in 25
and when I get there
you're still there
you're still there
and you make that special
noise of recognition
"b*pppphhhhhhh"*

so   we feed you mints and
carrots and apples
all your favourite things
and afterwards
the vet hands me your headcollar
and lead rope
and it's Valentines Day

and I'm driving home alone
my thumb brushing
over the brass buckle of your
best headcollar
your leather high days and holidays headcollar
and I'm beginning to understand that this
this is going to be
my Valentine's Day memory.

THAT WAS THE AND THIS NOW

At 18 I was careless;
let things slip through my fingers, pretty boys,
opportunities, a fabulous Biba frock,
confident that around the corner was a bigger,
better, shiny thing.

At 58, things still slip through my fingers,
arthritis clawing at my joints.
I'm losing my grip
and around this corner is
probably another corner.

At 18, in the room, in the squatted house,
on the street that nestled beneath the 3 tower blocks,
I filled the space with mirrors, papered the walls
with pages torn from the glossy magazines that Jem
stole so stylishly from the better department stores.

On days where there was not much going on,
we recreated those photos, expressed dissatisfaction,
but each of us secretly
a little in love with our own reflection.

At 58, there are days when I don't recognise the
woman who smiles hesitantly at me from plate glass
windows.

At 18 I was all about brazen presence,
walking through the market at 6am,
grey fedora hat,
men's vest slashed just below my breasts,
no bra and on my feet workmen's boots,

spray painted silver.

At 58 in my sensible dog walking coat
and my sensible dog walking shoes and
my sensible dog walking hat,
I am almost not here.

The boys who congregate on the park
to smoke weed are solicitous
when they spill from their bench onto the path,
"mind" says one,
"that lady needs to get by".

At 18 I knew everything I would ever need to know,
at 58, I tentatively offer these 3 truths;
dogs are better than hot water bottles,
you cannot own enough pairs of reading glasses,
and never take a good night's sleep for granted.

[5]
The Chi Chi Trilogy

MORE AND MORE I FIND MYSELF THINKING ABOUT CHI CHI THE PANDA - Part 1

It is the 1970s and the TV is black and white, there are colour TVs of course, but they still have a black and white one and sometimes that's a problem.

Sometimes when other children come around, they notice. Notice the TV, notice the holes in the carpet in the hallway, notice the saucepan instead of a kettle. But pandas work well in black and white.

It is the first time that she can remember actually watching the grown-up news, properly watching, not just waiting for it to finish and she sees the panda being carried down the steps of an aeroplane.

Weeks pass by and the panda story still fills the news. Chi Chi the panda has come all the way from China, she is a present from China. But not a present you get to keep yourself. She is a present for everyone.

Whenever she is on TV, there are always men in suits and the kind of hats dads wear when they go to work. A famous architect has designed her new home at London Zoo. London Zoo is in London which is a long way away from where they live.

For Christmas, the child asks for a panda. Really, she wants Chi Chi or at least the chance to go all the way to London to see the real Chi Chi. She does get a small fluffy black and white bear, she calls it Chi Chi. Plans to make a zoo home for her out of a cardboard box on the day after Boxing Day when they have nothing special to do.

She also receives: a Famous Five book, a selection box, a Wade Whimsy china rabbit, a new swimming costume, a charm for her charm bracelet - she has nine now and wears the bracelet all day on Christmas Day.

On Christmas Day evening, when the adults are opening a bottle of wine and all the nice Quality Street have been eaten, she lies quietly on her bed and strokes the bear's soft fur and whispers her name out loud,

Chi Chi,
Chi Chi,
Chi Chi.

MORE AND MORE I FIND MYSELF THNKING ABOUT CHI CHI THE PANDA – Part 2

The woman is being driven through London in a
Triumph Spitfire in a heat wave
it is sometime in the 90s

The car is not hers   the man is not her husband
even the year does not feel like her year

But the child   shoehorned into a space
not really big enough for anything larger than an
overnight bag
the child is most definitely hers

And the child is the reason for this trip
this jaunt   this Sunday afternoon educational outing

They are driving through London
to the Natural History Museum
to look at dinosaurs and polar bears
to press buttons and read tiny labels
they are going to have fun

The husband   the car   the A to Z
and a possibly misjudged Vivienne Westwood frock
are all on loan
borrowed from a friend who childless herself
does not quite see that a museum in August
may not be fun
they may not have fun

The man has never been to a museum with a child
he is not prepared for the whirlwind of movement

the restless gallop from thing to thing
the urgency of what's next

What's next?

The child sees the gift shop
latches onto a leopard head hat   furry   fully lined
designed for winter day
it is a ridiculous item when the sun
has made the car seats so hot
that the mother has spent the whole drive
lifting her thighs away from heat
hoping that this wriggling will not be mis-read
by the borrowed husband
in this borrowed car

The tearoom is in the basement
cool   green tiled   surprisingly deserted
and there   by the entrance is a panda
a stuffed panda in a glass display case

Even the child stops for a moment
and then walks up to the case
and looks carefully at what's inside
a slightly discoloured stuffed animal
a wall of black and white photos
and a small pyramid of
sun-faded soft toys

The woman joins her and then realises
that this is not just *a* panda
this is Chi Chi *the* panda
this is the panda from her childhood
her first memory of watching the grown-up news

the not-husband   is standing next to her   he shakes
his head
"Sad" he says *"Poor animal,*
on her own for so many years"

He and the child head towards the counter
queuing   looking at cake
both eyeing up the very pink ones
with many many smarties on top

Heat hits hard as they hit the pavement
child impervious   insists on wearing
the leopard headed hat

They drive away   to return the husband
the car   the A to Z and the frock
to their rightful owner

The only evidence of the woman's silent tears
are tiny water-damage spots on the silk
on the left sleeve of the borrowed dress.

CHI CHI GOING HOME – Part 3

I don't go out much anymore,
the light hurts my eyes, my old bones ache.
I am tired of the whoops, the shouts each time I appear.
I stay inside. The fact is well known,
a sign outside my enclosure prepares the public
for disappointment.

There is nothing to see here, not for you, not for
me. I have lived in this concrete approximation of
my home for 14 years.
Really there is nothing to see here, move on, move on.

It is summer, or what they call summer, sticky, hot,
the smell of fatty food in the air.

These are the only summers I remember clearly, but
when I sit in the dark, my back against the wall,
I can remember another time,
a time of cool green, the taste of fresh bamboo,
a vivid moment of crunch in my mouth.

The memory teases me, not quite caught, not ready
to be pinned down, examined, understood.

It's gone quiet now.
The constant drone of voices is over.
All I can hear is the murmur
of far-away traffic and of course my
own heart, not beating as strongly as it used to,
a little hesitant now,
a tiny pause between each beat,
each breath.

The keeper stays.
My breath's ragged now,
each heartbeat an effort,
the pauses longer
between each gasp.

The jungle thread begins to pull me back.
I feel the dappled sunlight against my fur.

I am going home.

[6]

To Do And Not To Do

I REMEMBER EVERYONE I HAVE EVER SLEPT WITH

1. I remember everyone I have ever slept with, even though I may have forgotten many of their names.

2. I remember the first time and afterwards, a shame faced entry into a sitting room where everyone knew our business.

3. I remember the last time with R, with nothing left to say, we took refuge under the duvet on a wet September day.

4. I remember sharing a bed with B, she carefully placed pillows down the centre line, a demarcation of distance, of decency and decorum.

5. I remember the man who would knock on my door at midnight and fool that I was, I would always let him in.

6. I remember spooning against A, his aubergine skin against mine, so dark it made my Irish whiteness glow in the soft light of my bedroom.

7. I remember sunny afternoons with J, lolling on a grubby mattress on the floor, we stuck out feet out of the window to cool ourselves and waved them at passers-by.

8. I remember another J, in a tent where we pressed our hands against each other's mouths so that we would not wake the other campers.

9. I remember, drunk on cava and sun, sharing a bed with my mother, we talked and giggled until the children, over-tired and fractious, told us to shut up and go to sleep.

10. I remember the stone-cold dyke, sprawled across my pillows, fully dressed as she watched me through half closed, calculating eyes.

11. I remember sleeping with A in a tipi and waking to find snowflakes drifting across our sleeping bag.

12. I remember a caravan in Norfolk and a small child pretending to be asleep while waiting for Christmas morning.

13. I remember dozing with the un-named Greenham women while we waited for daylight and yet another eviction.

14. I remember N's bed, so dipped and broken that we rolled together into an inevitable embrace, blaming fate and bad carpentry.

15. I remember sleeping with an almost famous comedian who insisted on leaning his double bass case at the foot of my bed. It loomed over us all night.

16. I remember New Year's Eve 1999, D threw pillows at my head when I talked in my sleep.

17. I remember M's home-made bed – 6 feet off the floor, we slept like over-sized birds in a wooden nest.

18. I remember a man who woke me to tell me that my cats were staring at him.

19. I remember sharing a bed with my sister, we slept top to tail, whispering and watching the flames die down in the bedroom grate.

20. I remember another R. We would listen to the shipping forecast late at night and he, claiming to be a sailor, would tell me tales of the sea, in retrospect, I see that many of these stories were fictions.

21. I remember M who in my freezing flat, wore his badly darned yellow jumper as some defence against the cold.

22. I remember a cat, who while I slept, gave birth to three tabby kittens.

23. I remember A who swore me to secrecy.

24. I remember the night I lured a model home and the look of disbelief on the faces of those left in the club who watched us leave.

25. I remember the Husky dog. As the night went on, she would move herself further and further up the bed, until, finally, her head would rest on a pillow, face staring into mine.

26. I remember small bear, wearer of tiny knitted trousers to stop his sawdust innards leaking.

27. I remember staggering home from a dentist, mouth full of blood and H who lay on top of the blanket, patting my hand until the pain killers kicked in.

28. All, many, some of these may be true, untrue, mis-remembered.

A NAMING OF PARTS

Your feet, bare, brown,
gritty with memory of sand and salt,
driving home after a seaside day.

At night,
my breath on the nape of your neck,
most vulnerable of all skin,
inviting confidences.

The scar on your belly,
my tongue traces the ghosts
of stitching.
I bite you, just enough to make you wince.

Wrists too large for me to circle with my fingers,
curiously hairless,
the skin there softer than your hand.

The dent in your nose,
bone broken in a life before I knew you.

Your balls, strange fruit, cool to my touch,
fitting exactly in a palm.
Their weight a known certainty.

Shoulder blades like bird wings,
sharp against my breasts when I lie behind you.

The curve of your spine,
arching towards me
as I play out each vertebra in turn.

Your nipples stiffening
with just my out breath
as I whisper your name into your chest.

The smell of you,
of musk and sweat and sex and
cheap cigarettes and expensive cologne.

I name your parts, a mapping,
sense-memory,
to keep you real,
to keep you here.

STRATEGIES TO A SUMMER STORM

Make no mistake, this is a snow day, sans snow.
A day when all bets are off, routines abandoned,
rhyme and rhythm lost.

This is not a day for useful enterprise, cupboard mining,
tax returning or self-improvement.

Before it breaks, before the s*turm* and *drang,*
stand and wait, wait at the window,
on a balcony, in a garden.
Wait in air so leaden with promise, with threat.

Wait.

Light a cigarette and watch the smoke hang heavy,
familiar tobacco scent cutting across a hint of metal,
electricity in the air.

The first flash, first fork is a signal.

Gather together small children,
pets and adults of a nervous disposition
on a life raft of duvets on the largest double bed.

It is permissible to collect extra pillows,
soft toys and snacks of a comforting nature
to ensure survival on this journey.

Priority places should be allocated to those
who can remember the techniques
for calculating the exact distance of the storm
from your roof top.

This calculation can contribute to the primary
numeracy curriculum and therefore,
this storm day is technically
a learning day.

Relax.

No food or drink consumed on a storm day
has any calories, fat or sugar content,
but choose carefully to ensure that all snacks
celebrate the spirit of summer storm.

Consider rum, hard bread, small fish.
If all else fails, select crisps,
conveniently packaged in water-proof bags.

Tell stories of storms passed, remember to embellish.

The horse hit by lightning,
it's metal shoes quadrilateral conductors.
The man drowned when the stream became a river,
became a torrent, became the sea.
Mr Noah, Mrs Wolfe.

Be kind to those who become fearful, they are right,
the gods are angry.
Do not share the statistics
of the likelihood of lightning strike.

It will not help.

Exile, exile immediately, anyone,
who peering into the sky, suggests that
"It seems to be clearing up"

This is a day to catastrophise,
to watch the world wash away,
street by street.

Eventually, you will have to succumb
to the irresistible rhythm of rain on roof.
Open the door, a deep breath,
give yourself up to the storm.

Stand and wave a fist at Thor
and all the gods
whose names you have forgotten.

Or

If you are less heroic, more self-conscious,
Sing quietly to yourself
"I'm singing in the rain,
just singing in the rain,
what a glorious feeling".

And as the words peter out,
find a puddle to stamp in.

12 THINGS YOU FIND AT BUS STOPS

1. A fox, eyes glittering, reflecting back in the headlights of the few cars that pass at 3am. He sits upright, primly at the front of a non-existent queue, for all the world as if he is waiting to catch the next bus to somewhere more interesting than this street of shuttered shops and dark terraced houses.

2. A dog lead and collar, red leather, small studs on the collar. The lead is looped neatly around the timetable post, secure, safe, no possibility of the dog slipping free, running blindly into the traffic, tied with care, with love. The absence of dog feels somehow more real in the half light of almost dawn.

3. A pair of 'fuck me' shoes, red patent leather, impossible heels. Owner, feet on fire, insteps throbbing, a plaster dug out from the deepest recesses of a tiny bag, failing to cover the blistered heel, falling into the bus stop and in a moment of loathing, slipping the shoes off.

4. A thermos flask and a Tupperware container, containing one triangle of ham sandwich. The sandwich is neat, cut with a sharp knife, white sliced bread, ham, butter, a man's sandwich. The thermos flask is elderly with a green checked pattern, fading into autumnal yellow.

5. A book, paperback, well used, pages turned down, spine starting to break. *'Men are from Mars, Women are from Venus'*.

6. One pearl earring, delicate, expensive, the pearl set in gold. It is shining in the streetlights. In the morning,

pecked by disappointed pigeons and pushed by busy work time feet, it will have rolled into the gutter and be lost among fast food wrapper and sodden leaves.

7. A mobile phone, fallen from a pocket and now under a seat. Later it will ring, but there will be no-one here to hear it.

8. A woman, hair and most of her face hidden, covered by niqab. Her heavy eye make-up is running, a trail of glittery green which vanishes into the heavy fabric. A tear falls from her eyes, her veil is soddening from crying.

9. A pair of false teeth.

10. A drunk man, half asleep and at his feet, wide awake, a chicken.

11. Two girls sit back-to-back on the red plastic chairs at the night bus stop. They lean into each other, sharing body heat. One is half asleep, eyes almost closed. She is humming the last track they heard at the club, still lost in music and the smell of sweat and fading perfume on her partner's skin.

12. The pantomime horse, drooping now, weighed down by the heat of fake fur and tired of trying to talk through the mesh of the horse head. The front hopes that the north bound bus will come first and that he can convince the back end to come back to his place.

THE WOMAN LISTS WHAT HAS BEEN LOST

1. A husband lost on a winters' day when waking she looked and saw a stranger's face on the pillow next to hers. The losing took more planning, more time, more effort than seemed possible once the decision had been made.

2. A grey velveteen rabbit, sewn by her grandmother, its button eyes, slightly uneven, giving it a constantly surprised expression. Left on a number 82 bus and never handed in, despite her insistence that her mother called at the lost property office week after week. It was years before she gave up hope of its return.

3. A diamond ring, borrowed without permission from the other grandmother, worn to impress a man who might have become her husband, but didn't. Her grandmother's dementia saved her from the shame of ever admitting this theft.

4. A lipstick, pillar box red, the one worn when she feared invisibility, a statement colour. A lipstick more exciting than she felt she could ever be. Its loss was somewhat of a relief, allowing her to embrace pale rose, a more fitting shade.

5. A cat, black and white, 5 years old. For years afterwards, she would carefully examine any similarly coloured animal until one day she realised that the cat, her cat, would be long dead.

Right Hand

1. A friend, a friendship that lasted through school and college and small children and no sleep and no money but slipped away, quietly, almost unnoticed when there was nothing left to complain about anymore.

2. A car, but only briefly, in those days when life seemed to consist of lists and tasks and don't-forgets. Parked on a day when her head felt so full that there was space for nothing else. A patient attendant walked from floor to floor with her until the car was found.
No longer lost.

3. A t-shirt, out-sized, fabric softened by years of washing to become the perfect sleeping garment. Lost, madly, mysteriously within her own home. Some days, she opens a drawer, digs into a cupboard, and is momentarily convinced that today will be the day when as mysteriously as it vanished, it will return.

4. A key, not her own, a key to someone else's house. She kept it, hanging uselessly on her own key ring, even though she never planned to open that door again.

5. A school duffle coat, bottle green, bought to grow into and finally, after several foiled attempts – returned from the bus stop, returned from the corner shop, returned from the bridge over the canal, thrown by Andrew Snell into the same canal. He believed it to be bullying, she wanted to kiss him with gratitude.

Left Foot

1. Her flat stomach, lost slowly, gradually. Baby 1, baby 2, a weakness for chocolate biscuits eaten noiselessly straight from the packet. Middle age, middle spread. She misses the taut flesh, but not enough to do anything about it.

2. A black thong, expensive, lacey, frivolous, worn for the man who gave her the key, also lost. For weeks afterwards, she tortured herself, imagining the underwear dropped from her bag in front of a colleague, a neighbour, her husband. She examined faces for knowing expressions, but nothing changed and finally she relaxed. Felt safe.

3. The collected poems of Sylvia Plath – shunted from bag to bag, dependent on her outfit, a talisman against boredom in the days before touch screens and I-things. She considered buying another copy but has found herself satisfied with "Take a Break" and "Hello" magazines.

4. A job, one to which she was so unsuited that she expected to lose it every day, practiced appropriate expressions of regret, dismay, made sure that she kept nothing important, irreplaceable in her desk drawers, just in case. The actual loss was something of an anti-climax after all.

5. Her virginity, it weighed heavily on her 16-year-old self and she gave it up happily to Nigel, he of the moped and the racing green hand knitted jumper. In retrospect, she wonders if he also lost his virgin status during their inept fumbling's in his mother's bed.

Right Foot

1. A breast and appropriately a right breast, enumerated on this right foot. She thought she would miss it more than she did, but by the time it went, she could look at it only with loathing, betrayer, mutant, mutating. No real loss at all.

2. Her youth, it seemed to leave her in one single day. She went to bed and woke, middle aged, as if the fairies had stolen it while she slept. She searches for it, in mirrors, in perfumed pots and jars. It has remained, defiantly, lost.

3. Hope, etched on her lips, permanently downward turning now, even when she smiles. The ghost of loss bleeding through.

4. A lost child, birthday still remembered but distantly, maths needed to work out the date. Sometimes overlooked until the day is half, two thirds, three quarters done, but then recalled, the day paused and then the memory put away for another year.

(Stop, stop now, focus on the last toe, the smallest, nail painted, soft pink – an easy loss, nothing loss)

5. A five-pound note, a small amount, inconsiderable, unimportant, perhaps not lost at all, perhaps put away, hidden, safe against a rainy day.

GRIM LITTLE THINGS

Grim

little

things

Snail slime across the pillow,
heading not towards the windowsill and away,
but downwards, towards the tangle of duvet and sheets.

That moment, with eyes still half closed,
you swing your feet out of bed and your toes
find something wet, soft and still just slightly warm.

Sniffing milk to test for freshness,
the almost-solidity of turn,
throat gagging on smell alone.

The crowded bus, the man too close,
stale sweat imperfectly masked by cheap deodorant,
his (at least to you) unwelcome erection
jabs against your hip at every speed bump.

The way a colleague chews her lunch,
mouth open, a whale seeking krill
and all the time you cannot tear your eyes away,
mastication and conversation.

A used dressing, plaster, still damp, sticky,
viscous and dropped by some stranger
into your wheelie bin.

A lipstick left, inadvertently,
to melt on a sunny windowsill.

A bloodied thumb print, just the one,
off centre on a downstairs light switch.

Chickens, necks yellowed,
hanging by their greying feet
in the make-shift halal butcher's storefront.

A toenail, blackened, hanging by a single thread.
When walking, you feel it move,
shift under woollen socks, but fear the final loss,
the display of pink unready flesh.

Coppers sticky from over-handling
pressed into your palm,
exact change for 20 cut price cigarettes.

A windscreen splattered,
with the flying dead and the noise
the wipers make removing the crispy bits.

Undercooked quiche, onion floating
in a thin soup of egginess.

A pug, eyes popping, pink onesie
and a matching hot pink collar.

Knuckles cracking, slow, deliberate,
preparation and then the silence.

That Nokia ringtone
Da da da …dadad da…dada da da.

Any envelope with any Government dept stamp.

Cells mutating under a microscope.

An ageing neck.

And on
and on and on and on.

WHY I RAN AWAY....VOICES OF THE DISAPPEARED

One day I ran away to join the circus,
but there wasn't any circus, so I just ran away instead.

I didn't come off the motorway at the usual exit,
I just kept driving until I ran out of petrol and then
I sat in the car with my head on the steering wheel
while I waited for something to happen.

Before I walked away, I cleaned the bathroom,
even the bits that didn't show, I knew that everyone
would think badly enough of me, I didn't want
them to think I was dirty too.

I sat at work, adding up figures and suddenly
realised that I hadn't managed
one act of significance in my life.

I ran before it all came crashing down,
the sense of relief was immense.

I couldn't bear the way she looked at me,
couldn't bear the way she tried to keep
the children quiet, convinced myself
that they would all be better off if I wasn't there.

I tried to pretend that nothing had changed,
that I was still the same person.
On the nights when I woke, covered in sweat,
my wife cowering in a corner of the bedroom,
keeping that pretence going seemed impossible.

I couldn't get her to shut up, couldn't stop her
asking for more and more.
I walked out early one morning.

I didn't look back.

I ran away the day before the building society
repossessed the house.

I walked out, and nobody noticed.

He broke my heart and made a mockery
of my carefully constructed little life,
so, I went in search of a better one.

When I lost my job, I knew I should go home
to face the music, but I caught a train instead.

I realised that I only stayed to give the dog a home,
so I left and took the dog with me.

The more I owned, the more it all seemed a burden,
I dreamt of being weightless, so I took the smallest bag
we had and even that seemed too much to own.

I wanted less history, to become someone different,
to reinvent myself. I sat on a bus,
considering and discarding new first names.

I wanted someone to miss me.

I couldn't find a way of going back, so I didn't,
but I wish I could, sometimes.

I ran away because I was too afraid to stay.

[7]

Newer Poems

AND COUNTING

At 12 my daughter starts to spread her wings
her chosen companions on shopping trips
her mates not me
so there are rules
stay together   don't talk to boys
if all else fails or you're frightened
and things fall apart
go find someone in a uniform
they're there to help you
White privilege

In a clapped-out car
seen many better days
and a brake light that flickers on
and off and on
I get pulled over and I smile
ratchet up my accent a notch or two
invent a wholly fictitious husband
who fails to fix the simplest thing
waved on and told to get it sorted soon
White privilege

Our house burgled
every room ransacked
every drawer undone
the police arrive   solicitous
armed with window stickers
and contact details for a charity
that gives support
the officer strategically chooses to ignore

the stench of weed that sneaks from under
my adult daughter's door
White privilege

And years ago
burdened with babies and bags
a buggy whose back wheel sticks
I fail to see that my child has
helped herself to a small plush bear
until halfway home
so of course we turn
ignore the chorus of wails and tears
in the shop they're charmed
insists she keeps the toy
White privilege

So intent on conversation
with a man
I hoped might be a lover
we left the coffee shop
didn't pay our bill
but no pavement pounding pursuit for us
White privilege

Lost on a leafy lane
we stopped to ask the gardening guy for help
unsure   he summoned his wife
from deep indoors
and asked how our holiday was going
recommended a nearby pub
that welcomes dogs
White privilege

Never asked where I come from
never asked where I really   really
really come from
no badly disguised surprise at my use of words
or my ability to solve a cryptic crossword clue

White privilege   and on   and on   and on.

A DEAR JOHN LETTER TO THE DIET INDUSTRY

Oh the lies you told me, the lies you sold me
first diet   age thirteen
clearly misunderstanding the science   but not society
told that grapefruit magically melts fat away
so we girls sat at the far end of the playing fields
declared ourselves too full to move
and in the afternoon at double maths
we gnawed on pencils
just to give our mouths something to do

Lie 1
My worth was only measured by a diminishing return
a diminuendo   a scaling down of self
less is always more you told me

Lie 2
When I could have been reading anything
anything at all
you gave me a book that told me everything
every food reduced to numbers too
a crème egg contains 177 calories
and in fairness I had to look this up
no longer burnt into my memory

Lie 3
You said your body will betray you but it's easily fooled
so drink water by the litre
bite down on shrapnel-sharp ice slivers
hunger isn't real   it's boredom   keep busy
clean your teeth   go running   learn to knit
learn to close your mind to what your body says it needs

Lie 4
Food is not for fun you said
I filled my fridge with food labelled sin free
cottage cheese and carrots   fizzy water/diet coke
calorie accountancy
as though eating could put my soul
in mortal jeopardy

Lie 5
You gave me useful aphorisms
told me to write them on the pad that you provided
decorated with your big business logos/online support
I wrote them on my mirror
Nothing tastes as good as skinny feels
A moment on your lips   a lifetime on your hips
No-one loves a quitter
each morning started with a litany of loathing

Lie 6
You told me that my ideal weight
existed on a chart   my BMI
a measurement of value/validity and virtue
still the scales didn't fall from my eyes

Lie 7
And when I failed again
you always had the answer
no carbs after 5
no carbs after 3
no carbs
keto   caveman   intermittent fasting
if it didn't work – the fault was always mine

Lie 8
That this all mattered, really mattered
so we sat each week
wearing our lightest clothes
on borrowed chairs in borrowed halls
eyes not meeting   public shame of weight gained
managing to maintain
secretly hating loser of the week

And so dear diet industry
we are done   just decades of your work to get undone
and yes quite frankly
it's not me   it's you.

A MANIFESTO ON AGEING

I am my own manifesto
a tiny revolution that will not be televised
I dream of hiring town criers
armed with loudhailers to stand on
commuter platforms and disrupt the narrative of youth
"don't mind the gap".

I imagine crowd-funded billboards
on gridlocked motorway junctions
joyous images
of ordinarily ageing bodies.

We are not invisible.

This body wears every week and month
of its 61 years with pride and defiance.

This body refuses to go gentle
into that night of beige neutrality.

This body says I am not in need of fixing
with procedures and plastic surgery
and tiny pots of over-priced creams.

I am my mapped experience
unrepentant uncoloured hair
skin that's lost the ping of youth
knuckles that have undergone an arthritic sea change.

I share these images of an older woman
without manipulation   photoshop or filter

A subversive statement
a celebration of the inevitable
without apology or excuse.

Join me   make an everyday statement
of presence and validity.

DEAD CLEAN – FOR VERA

(in the language of domestic cleaners, a dead clean can refer to a final clean when a client has died, but it also refers to a clean after a client has moved into residential care – the job is dead to us)

And some truisms trip off the tongue
but really   it does feel
as if you have just stepped out
for a moment or two
or more likely   knowing you
that you will suddenly appear on the stairs
stepping carefully sideways   rail gripped tight
fixing me with a glare
demanding to know what I'm doing here
at such an ungodly hour
and on a Sunday too

If I don't look too carefully
it all seems fine
new jigsaw started
pieces of sea and sky separated
into saucers   little pools of blue
against the heavily varnished dining table
a wedding gift   from sixty years ago
back when things were made to last

The fruit bowl's still full   but
when I touch the melon's greying skin
it collapses into itself
releases a flurry of feasting fruit flies
and I wave my hands in front of my face
fend them away

first movements in this house   for weeks

I follow the trail of something off
discover the room of stockpiled food
delivered when the world closed down
and your mind closed down as well
with nothing to keep you
anchored anymore

And there are things
that you would hate for me to see
discarded underwear
an unmade bed   false teeth
and a lipstick   peachy pink
your make up bag was left behind

The sink's still full of washing up
as though you have lost
our weekly argument
"leave it" I would say
"it's my job"
the water is scummy   brown and stagnant
I take a deep breath
squirt bleach   begin

Restoration work
the righting of a house
back into a home
as if you really have just stepped outside
to pick apples from your tree
are coming back
and soon
jigsaw to be finished
lipstick to be applied.

THE MAN IN THE PINSTRIPED SUIT

The man in the pinstriped suit
is going to the circus
but shush, it's a self-made surprise
his interview-worthy shined-up shoes
hide a pair of hot pink socks
in his pocket is a ticket
in his briefcase there are buns
just in case that there are elephants
he really hopes that there are elephants

the woman with the bags and the to-do list
that's never done
is dreaming of being on a trampoline
instead her fingers bounce
against her knees
she sees herself perform perfect parabolas
and as she does she sheds
the weight of being right and proper

the pensioner in the pac-a-mac
beige waterproof   rain-ready
is really on the catwalk at Milan
unsteady in the highest heels
struts her stuff and smiles
at clicking camera lenses
pretends for just a moment
she could be Kate Moss
and then checks her purse for keys and trolley fob

the man in the white van dreams of autobahns
empty roads   driving to the soundtrack
of Kraftwerk or Gary Numan

but being human
he plots the route he needs to take
undaunted by diversions
and routes now closed
steals time at stop lights   smiles
cranks the windows open
shares his music with the world outside

my friend   the reader
travels inside his head
walking on Dubliner paved streets
following in Stephen's steps
on Sandymount Strand
recreates that day with Bloom and all the others
knows a city where he's never been
as well as the back of his own hand

other people's dreaming is as
secret as their sleeping.

TEA NO SYMPATHY

Well of course those sorts of men were there
when I was small
I saw them
multi-overcoated even in summer
a hint of body   woodsmoke
and something else that lingered long
when they were gone
"spare a couple of bob for a cuppa missus"
defiantly pre-decimal
and my mother who knows a thing or two
about how poverty
sneaks up to bite you in the butt
would bustle us by
terrified that even contact could cause contamination
takes us back to that place
where we were grateful
for those food parcels from the nuns

but
when did it become ok for minimum wage workers
under order to pour water on the
possessions of the dispossessed
when did it become ok for someone
to design the perfect spike to un-bench a bench

and Nikki's tiny   takes up hardly any space
and that's all good
because it's what she doesn't have   some space
the daily ritual of folding and unfolding the sofa bed
in her in-laws sitting room
and its cosy for a night or two
but when your pre-schooler has never slept alone

the novelty is long worn off

and when did it become ok for someone
with a clipboard to tell her that
she's not overcrowded enough
to tell her that she's not homeless enough
when did it become ok for Nikki and her mates
to talk about a one-bed flat
as though it was a unicorn
fabulous   mythic
and always out of reach

and Ted's no stranger to danger
risked life and limb a lifetime ago
in bombed out buildings in the blitz
risked life and limb again last week
scrabbling in the attic
no cash just a stash of rugs and blankets put away
against a rainy day
and Ted's got a plan he says
one room winter living
one bar fire used sparingly
tartan picnic flask pressed back to service

but
when did it become ok for bloated billionaires
to give us budgeting advice
when did it become ok to say you heat or eat
Hobson's choice made real

and my Facebook feed is full of food banks
posting needs
toiletries, toothpaste
sanitary protection, pain relief
and in the queue there are people

who will not meet your eyes
40% of food bank users are in work   40%
as truth as tasteless
as hard to swallow as those charity biscuits
from the sisters

but
when did it become ok for this to be
a photo opportunity for Tory wanna-bes
when did it become ok to pay so low
the smallest slip will send you off the cliff
hurtling into hunger

"spare a couple of bob for a box of tea bags missus."

MIRROR IMAGE

The mirror shows me as my mother now
and as I stare jolted by a face
that shows the years of living
I run my fingers across the braille of everyday
blind sighted   bas relief   basic relief
of still being here

Behind this reflection
there stands that line of women who gifted me
hair that silvered early
and finger joints misshapen into something close to
but not quite the hands I used to own

Can't still the clock so why not   just stop
embrace the place where I live now
age needs no apologies   no muffling in clothes
deemed suitable   a symphony in beige and taupe

This body is its own revolution
a micro manifestation of change
I stare into the camera   unashamedly myself
the ghosts of other women
line up behind my shoulders.

VIGIL

Breath
and
pause
and pause

so
we both learn forward
each take a hand to hold
choreography seamless now

and we no longer know what face to wear
when you breathe again
no one talks about the dullness of the death bed
exhausting
and surprisingly soporific
we have both dropped into sleep at different times
jerked awake
wearing the commuter's look of lost confusion
scared she may have missed her stop

breath
and
pause
and pause
and pause

when we're alone
I talk to you
conversations we've had a hundred times
the gardens
yours and mine
the dogs

upstairs now
confused
dozing on a single bed

breath
pause
and pause
and pause
and pause
and pause

for something else to do
to fill this time
I mimic your breathing
learn that living lungs
need something more

simply make myself a little giddy

breath
pause
and pause
and pause
and pause.

THESE PETS ARE IN THE WRONG PLACES

1. Owning an iguana is the closest I have ever come to
    ownership of a bonsaied dinosaur
    this one is four foot long from tip of studded tail
    to ancient stony face

    I have created a home of sorts in the previously
    perfectly usable understairs cupboard
    she entertains herself by launching at the glass to scare
    the cats as they creep by
    the house seems full of ghostly chirps
    from long dead crickets delivered living
    and boxed in corrugated cardboard

2. The train slows   shudders, and stalls on the track
    in a space neither journey nor destination
    so there is time   so much time
    to see the dogs   one slumped
    trapped in that place between rails and sidings
    we are too far away to know if it is dead
    or simply injured
    the other sits upright   ears upright
    face to the sky looking for
    something   someone   anything
    memory sharp as a snap-shot
    but somehow lost   buried   long forgotten
    resurfaces with perfect clarity
    in conversation decades later

3. On a holiday in Paris which by day two is already
   making concrete the unstable foundations
   of this marriage
   our room faces onto a balcony
   carelessly wrapped in chicken wire
   a roofless cage
   it contains a dog
   completely contains a dog
   nose touches one end   tail the other
   it stands or sits   stares at nothing
   I stare at it   we pass the day

4. It seems impossible
   but then again   it was the 1970s
   and more importantly the Black Country
   and somewhere amongst
   a ramshackle selection of sheds
   stuffed with second hand furniture
   one shed housed a bear
   a live bear   admittedly
   not a big bear   but still a bear
   the humanity at the core of me
   wants and needs this to be a misremembering

    the poet

    not so much

5. The man in the pet shop says
    I can have her for eighty-five quid
    and I know that she's a she because
    she's wearing a doll's party frock
    silver stars   and red nylon
    a handknitted cardigan because she feels the cold
    her face   the size of my palm
    I stretch out   to touch the wizened skin
    she holds my hand
    fingers so light their weight might be imaginary

    the monkey might have been imaginary

    On the market, mince for fifty pence a pound
    the queue for day old bread same length as
    the day before.

PIG

Yes I know you're kind and clever
clean and curious
but you are also delicious
a happy marriage of DNA and
decades of selective breeding
maybe on some other Earth
they've decided that dogs taste just as good
so there it's all
#pigsof Instagram
#pigletswearingonesies
#smileyfacesmileyfaceheartheartsmileyface
but here you are the siren song
for every fledgling vegetarian
best wake-up call for even the most
determined Sunday morning sleepy head
you're better than sliced bread
hey   you're better in sliced bread
no need for artifice
just a mug of builder's tea
three sugars and a blob of sauce

and if I could I'd raise and name
and nurture you myself
give you a death that's dignified
use up every scrap of you
say thank you for your sacrifice
but I can't because pigs are bloody big
and it would be the chicks again
bought for eggs and for the pot
but named and so lived out lives
of barren bone idleness

who knew that hens could live
for seven years
and in one case eight

so I won't hide behind euphemisms
you are not ham or gammon
pork or chop
you are pig and I salute you.

Cathi Rae is a poet and spoken word artist, somewhat accidentally living in the East Midlands.

Outside of poetry she is an older model, a sustainable stylist and a campaigner challenging the invisibility of older women. You can find her on Instagram @CathiRae

She teaches creative writing for adults and is a freelance educator and workshop facilitator.

She has an MA in Creative Writing from the University of Leicester and has recently been awarded a practice-led PhD in Poetry.

Which immediately after receiving she rushed off to work, cleaning a house...

Well, nothing changes.

www.ingramcontent.com/pod-product-compliance
Lightning Source LLC
Chambersburg PA
CBHW030307100526
44590CB00012B/557